To:

From:

ZONDERVAN

Stillness
Copyright © 2009 by Zondervan

Requests for information should be addressed to:
Zondervan, *Grand Rapids, Michigan* 49530

ISBN 978-0-310-82288-2

Design by Jody Langley

Printed in China

09 10 11 12 13 14 15 • 23 22 21 20 19 18 17 16 15 14 13 12 11 10 9 8 7 6 5 4 3 2 1

stillness

WONDER AND AWE

Viewing the heavens God has created is an inspiring exercise. Slip away one warm, clear night and throw a blanket on the ground. Lie there in the darkness, take in the broad expanse of the sky, and watch as dancing dots of brilliant light shimmer above, beneath and around the silver orb of the moon. In comparison to such a startling display, problems often appear small and inconsequential and possibilities great and unlimited.

In moments like these your heart is most receptive to God's still, small voice—the voice that comes from within and envelops you with a sense of joy and thankfulness, the voice that tells you that you are more important to him than the moon and all the stars. You are the crowning achievement of all God's creation.

Author Unknown

Be at rest once more, O my soul.

Psalm 116:7

Be still before the Lord.

Psalm 37:7

BE STILL

I love that Scripture. Sometimes in the franticness of my life, I just have to stop and repeat that Scripture to myself. Here's what I know: when we're racing through life at Daytona 500 speeds, jumping from one thing to another, we can't hear or feel him. We're too distracted by stress and distress. *Be still.* Just as the Scripture says. When we quiet ourselves, we will hear what God has to tell us. That's important, because from him comes the wisdom and guidance we need in everyday life. I wake up early every morning and lie in bed for a long while, talking to him in the darkness of the early dawn and asking him to speak back. Sometimes I go into my walk-in closet, where it is quiet and there is no television or phone, and get down on my face to pray.

Ronda Rich

The Lord will fight for you;
you need only to be still.

Exodus 14:14

THE UNHURRIED LIFE

Not long after moving to Chicago, I called a wise friend to ask for some spiritual direction. I described the pace at which things tend to move in my current setting. I told him about the rhythms of our family life and about the present condition of my heart, as best I could discern it. What did I need to do, I asked him, to be spiritually healthy?

Long pause. "You must ruthlessly eliminate hurry from your life," he said at last. Another long pause.

"Okay, I've written that one down," I told him, a little impatiently. "That's a good one. Now what else is there?" Another long pause.

"There is nothing else," he said.

John Ortberg

"For I know the plans I have for you," declares the LORD, "plans to prosper you and not to harm you, plans to give you hope and a future."

Jeremiah 29:11

LETTING GO

The practice of silence is the radical reversal of our cultural tendencies. Silence is bringing ourselves to a point of relinquishing to God our control of our relationship with him. Silence is a reversal of the whole possessing, controlling, grasping dynamic of trying to maintain control of our own existence. Silence is the inner act of letting it go.

M. Robert Mulholland Jr.

A CALMER FAITH

A calmer faith. That's the quiet place within us where we don't get whiplash every time life tosses us a curve. Where we don't revolt when his plan and ours conflict. Where we relax (versus stew, sweat, and swear) in the midst of an answerless season. Where we accept (and expect) deserts in our spiritual journey as surely as we do joy. Where we are not intimidated or persuaded by other people's agendas, but moved only by him. Where we weep in repentance, sleep in peace, live in fullness, and sing of victory.

Patsy Clairmont

I have stilled and quieted my soul.

Psalm 131:2

THE COLORS OF LIFE

I loved winter where I grew up in Scotland. It was quiet. After school I would head down to the ocean. I would sit there for a long time, enjoying the songs of the sea. Sometimes I would settle onto a rock, close enough to get splashed by the salty spray. I loved it. That was where I did my serious praying. Out there, surrounded by the wind and the water, I knew I served an awesome God.

Those winter days are part of who I am—a winter person. I love the reds and the yellows of the world, the brighter side, but there will always be a place in my heart for the grays and ebony shades of life.

Sheila Walsh

Make it your ambition to lead a quiet life.

1 Thessalonians 4:11

TAKE A CLUE FROM A SLOTH

Sloths are animals that really know the meaning of stillness. They spend between fifteen and twenty hours a day sleeping while hanging upside down from tree limbs in South American jungles. When sloths do move they make turtles look like road runners.

Lots of other animals on land and in the sea are able to remain perfectly motionless for hours on end waiting for prey to walk or swim by. All of these patient animals find mates, bear offspring, "work" at building homes and finding food, and more or less get all of their needs met without rushing. Obviously, God saw some value in stillness when he created these creatures, and perhaps there's a lesson here for humans. It's not in God's plan for anyone to live their life in a frenzy.

Steven Cole

The Lord says,
"In quietness and trust is your strength."

Isaiah 30:15

THE ART OF SERENITY

The spiritual art of serenity is an inner thing; it comes from the heart. It is perhaps the most sought-after art of all. Who doesn't want to be serene in the midst of chaos? The dictionary defines "serenity" as "tranquility," "calmness," "an undisturbed state." God's Word defines it as biblical "peace."

Joy is faith dancing; peace is faith resting. Faith in a God who doesn't make mistakes, who has the whole world in his hands—including my worried world—releases us to laugh at dark days and to dance in the rain. Where can we find joy in life itself with all its drama and pain? We find it in God.

Jill Briscoe

When I am afraid,
I will trust in you, O God.

Psalm 56:3

OVER THE EDGE

Mountain climbing isn't just about summiting pyramidal peaks. For many climbers, far greater challenges are presented by "big walls," vertical mountain faces hundreds, sometimes thousands, of feet high. Such big walls exist in Yosemite National Park in California, the Rockies in Colorado, and elsewhere around the world.

Climbers scale big walls by grasping tiny holds no wider than the thickness of this book and pulling themselves up by their fingers. For safety they pound metal eyebolts called pitons into the rock face and attach themselves to them with a rope.

Big walls are usually too big to climb in a day, so climbers carry a tent called a portaledge which cantilevers over the void and is anchored to the rock with pitons and rope. Climbing into the contraption requires slow, careful moves and, once inside, nearly complete stillness. Imagine you had a portaledge hung on your living room wall with a few bolts into the studs. But instead of a few feet between the tent and the floor there was 2,000 feet of space. Portaledges are no place for people who thrash in their sleep!

Living with such danger focuses climbers' minds and makes them aware of every move. The closeness of death produces a stillness that brings many of them closer to God. The climber must have trust in his or her mountaineering skills but must also trust that God will make sure the pitons hold the portaledge through the night.

Is your faith strong enough that you could enter a flimsy portaledge thousands of feet from the ground and go to sleep knowing God would take care of you?

Steven Cole

You will eat but not be satisfied;
your stomach will still be empty.

Micah 6:14

GULP IT DOWN

We suffer from what has come to be known as "hurry sickness." We will buy anything that promises to help us hurry. We worship at the shrine of the Golden Arches not because they sell "good food" or even "cheap food," but because it is "fast food." Even after fast food was introduced, people still had to park their cars, go inside, order, and take their food to a table, all of which took time. So we invented the drive-thru lane to enable families to eat in vans, as nature intended.

John Ortberg

There is a time for everything ... a time to be silent and a time to speak.

Ecclesiastes 3:7

WHO WE ARE WITH GOD

We tend to think of solitude as simply being alone. In the classical Christian spiritual tradition, however, solitude is in the silence of release, beginning to face our brokenness, our distortion, our darkness and beginning to offer ourselves to God at those points. Solitude is not simply drawing away from others and being alone with God. This is part of solitude. But more than this, it is being who we are with God and acknowledging who we are to ourselves and to God.

M. Robert Mulholland Jr.

WITHIN STILL WATERS

In the Indonesian islands where I grew up people feel an intimacy with the sea that goes far beyond eating the food it yields. When I got my first snorkel and mask at age six I took to the water like the fish who live in it. I was fascinated and wanted to explore deeper and deeper. By the time I was a teenager I was scuba diving.

Seas are usually only rough on the surface. Beneath the waves it is still and silent. For me, shutting out the world by diving underscores the fact that every one of us needs a way to bring stillness, solitude and silence to our lives. As I plumb the depths of God's silent world, and see all the varied and colorful creatures he has placed in the ocean, I come closer to him than I ever could on dry land.

Tamela DeKoster

There is the sea, vast and spacious,
teeming with creatures beyond number.

Psalm 104:25

THE INNER GAME

I grew up playing tennis with my dad and our house was filled with books about tennis. The best one was *The Inner Game of Tennis.* The author said, "Every game is composed of two parts, an outer game and an inner game. The outer game is played against an external opponent to overcome external obstacles, and to reach an external goal." To master the outer game, we must learn to swing a racquet. The outer game is what people see.

But there is another, more important game going on in the mind of the player. It is played against nervousness, doubt, and self-condemnation. It requires the offering of the will and the focus of the mind. Victories at the inner game are the source of all true joy and growth. The possibility of inner mastery is the highest reason why we play the game.

John Ortberg

The effect of righteousness will be quietness and confidence forever.

Isaiah 32:17

Time is but the stream I go a-fishing in.
I drink of it; but while I drink I see
the sandy bottom and detect how
shallow it is. Its thin current slides away,
but eternity remains.

Henry David Thoreau

SETTLE DOWN!

Nothing is unhurried these days. We wish we had thirty hours in every day, eight days in every week. There's never enough time. God says, "Be still and know me." Stop all this crazy running around. None of it matters as much as you think.

There's a great story in the New Testament about this kind of busyness. Mary and Martha have invited Jesus to dinner. Martha runs around getting everything prepared, while Mary simply sits and listens to Jesus. You can just imagine Martha's tone when she's had enough of being the kitchen slave, "Lord, don't you care that my sister has left me to do the work by myself? Tell her to help me!" (Luke 10:40). Jesus answered, "Mary has chosen what is better." The most important thing is to take time with God. The rest will fall into place.

Roz Stirling

God blessed the seventh day and made it holy, because on it he rested from all the work of creating that he had done.

Genesis 2:3

There remains then, a Sabbath—
rest for the people of God.

Hebrews 4:9

INTO THE DARKNESS

Editor's note: Jerry Sittser, a professor of religion at Whitworth College, lost his wife, daughter and mother in a tragic automobile accident. In his book, *A Grace Disguised*, he describes coming to terms with his loss.

I tried to reserve time and space in my life for solitude so that I could descend into the darkness alone. Late in the evening, well after the children were in bed, proved to be the best time for me. Mostly I sat in my rocking chair and stared into space, reliving the accident and remembering the people I lost.

This nightly solitude, as painful and demanding as it was, became sacred to me because it allowed time for genuine mourning and intense reflection. It also gave me freedom during the day to invest my energy into teaching and caring for my children. I struggled with exhaustion. But somehow I found the strength—God's gift to me, I think—to carry on despite getting so little sleep.

Jerry Sittser

After the suffering of his soul,
he will see the light of life.

Isaiah 53:11

"CAMPING" IN THE BASEMENT

My friends Al and Debbie lead hectic lives, what with three young children, a boisterous dog and a busy schedule of work and church activities. Debbie finds a bit of relax time in her weekly painting class at the university. But Al was becoming more and more frazzled until he hit upon an idea. He pitched a tent in the basement.

Al stocked the tent with a soft mattress, a blanket, some pillows, a reading light, his well-thumbed Bible and a concordance. When Al needs some time alone, he retreats to his tent. It's quiet and he can refresh his soul in solitude while getting to know God more intimately.

Vernon Perkins

*It is good to wait quietly
for the salvation of the Lord.*

Lamentations 3:26

Man bustles about, but only in vain.

Psalm 39:6

STILL THE TURBULENCE

Imagine taking a jar half-filled with soil and half-filled with water. When you shake the jar, turbulence mixes the soil and water, giving you a murky liquid.

In much the same way, the turbulence of life can easily scatter our thoughts and reduce our plans and priorities to disarray. Setting aside moments to be silent and still is crucial for the restoration of our souls. Because, just as the soil will settle to the bottom of the jar of water if left undisturbed, so will the turbulence in your life dissipate when your "jar" is no longer shaken.

Author Unknown

Search your hearts and be silent. Selah.

Psalm 4:4

SELAH!

A good novel can get your adrenaline going, leading you to turn pages faster and faster. Poetry has the opposite effect. It slows you down. The Psalms may not look like the poetry you're accustomed to as they don't include measured stanzas or patterns of rhyme. But the Psalms are filled with poetic expression of raw emotion and metaphor. That's why some of them include musical terms like Selah.

Selah means pause. During this pause, people would listen to a musical interlude or simply reflect on what had been sung by the psalmist. Selah was a kind of soul retreat written directly into the poem. So, Selah right now!

Author Unknown

Marriage should be honored by all.

Hebrews 13:4

CUDDLE TIME

How often are you really quiet and still when you're with your spouse? Usually, we're either doing something or saying something when we're around him or her. Couples need to pause and simply enjoy the closeness of their spouse without activity or words. Try climbing into a hammock together and swinging quietly in a summer breeze. Or share a blanket at the beach and watch the waves lapping at the sandy shore. Or sit together on the front porch on a dark, clear night with your arms around each other's waists, and glory in God's starry universe.

As you sit quietly together, think about all the little things you love about your spouse but hardly ever say. Then, after a while, break the silence and share your special thoughts.

Glenna Cress

PURR-FECT REST

If you have a pet in your life, take a few minutes from your busy day and enjoy what God has given you. Talk up a storm—pets are great listeners and they never give away your secrets. But do more than talking. Take a little vacation into your pet's world. Lie by the fire with your dog, slouch on the sofa with your cat, perch a chair near your bird's cage. Then let your pet lead the way, initiating affection and play.

If you don't have a pet, animals can still provide a retreat for your soul. Hang a bird feeder outside your window, visit a pond and feed the ducks and geese, or take a few minutes to watch the squirrels racing around the backyard.

Author Unknown

A kind man benefits himself.

Proverbs 11:17

Jesus went up on a mountainside to pray.

Mark 6:46

CLIMBING IN SILENCE

There is a lot about silence, solitude and stillness in the sport of high altitude mountain climbing. To begin with, achieving the summit is a solitary effort depending solely on putting one foot ahead of the other thousands and thousands of times. Unlike picking up a heavy object or pushing a stalled car, no one can help you. The higher you climb, the thinner the air, and the effort of breathing becomes the climber's main focus. There is an ever-present danger of falling to your death, of being struck by loose boulders falling from above, or being buried in thousands of tons of snow from an avalanche. Achieving the goal safely requires intense concentration. The climber literally "checks out" and focuses only on his or her body and mind.

The upper reaches of the "eight thousanders," mountains exceeding 8,000 meters or 26,240 feet, are quieter than you might suppose. Oh, there's wind and blowing snow sometimes, but at other times it is as still as still can be, and the vastness of the landscape adds to the effect.

Reaching the summit of many high mountains such as Everest requires several hours of climbing. Climbers typically arise at midnight or soon thereafter, and begin their ascent. This ensures that they can reach the summit and return to a safer lower elevation before dark that day. How can you climb a mountain in the dark? Much of the climbing on extremely high mountains does not involve scaling vertical walls like you see in sporting goods stores in the mall. On high mountains it can be more "horizontal" than you'd expect, and there are immense slopes that lead up gradually for miles. Picture climbing a sand dune and you'll get the idea.

Since high altitude climbing is such an intense, personal sport, climbers come to know themselves very well. With every step they are aware of every part of their body and soul, of the environment and universe. Many climbers say that, exhausted and deprived of oxygen, they experience hallucinations. Often, climbers say they feel there is someone slogging up the mountain beside them. And this companion climber is there throughout the most difficult times. This phantom climber is clearly God, and he reaches into the climber's heart and soul more deeply than can be imagined.

Summiting high mountains is a profoundly moving experience, a communion with God's power that few climbers will ever forget.

Steven Cole

THE QUIET FOREST

Some time ago I had a day of solitude in a forest preserve. I felt the kind of weariness of the flesh the writer of Ecclesiastes talked about. And I realized how strongly I had been living for certain achievements, and how I felt it as heaviness when they were not realized. I was caught up in my own trivial pursuits.

But I was in the kind of natural setting where it is hard to remain discontent for long. The chestnut trees and oaks and maples and sycamores were on fire with autumn colors in brilliant October sunshine. And something happened. I began to get free. I was somehow given the gift of sensing that God loved me. I began to feel again what a gift it was to be alive, on *this* earth, in *this* place, during *this* moment.

John Ortberg

All things are wearisome,

more than one can say.

Ecclesiastes 1:8

I will lie down and sleep in peace.

Psalm 4:8

COCOON

My friend Mike can be pretty crazy. For example, in college he started sleeping in a sleeping bag. Sheets and blankets were too much trouble, he said. Besides, Mike said, the sleeping bag enabled him to shut out the world so he could say his nightly prayers in complete solitude.

Mike was a bachelor, still sleeping in a sleeping bag, well into his thirties. Then he met Debbie at a church retreat. They clicked, then started dating, and Mike asked Debbie to marry him. She agreed on one condition: There'll be no sleeping bag in the marriage bed. "We'll find some other way to meet quietly with God," she said firmly. "Well, they do make double sleeping bags," Mike said meekly. "No!" Debbie replied.

Jerry Rickey

O Lord, I sat alone because
your hand was on me.

Jeremiah 15:17

NEVER ALONE

While many people will seek time with you today, God is waiting for that one-on-one time as well. If possible, find a place free of noise and other distractions. Settle into a comfortable position and ask God to direct your thoughts as you spend the next few moments focusing on him. These moments may refresh your mind and soul. They should also remind you that you are never alone. God is with you every moment of every day. In fact, one of the attributes that distinguishes God as God rather than as creature is his omnipresence. He is in all places at all times.

Author Unknown

ONE FOOT AT A TIME

Put down your work, step back from your computer, and put on your walking shoes. Go outside and start walking. Don't think about where you're going. Don't set a time when you have to be back. Just put one foot in front of the other.

Look around. What do you see? Take a deep breath. What do you smell? Stop and listen. What do you hear? Now listen to yourself. Is your mind starting to slow down, is your body beginning to relax? Keep walking until they do.

Most times, walking is merely a way to get from point A to point B. Start walking in a different way. Let your walking be intentional in its slower pace.

Author Unknown

He who walks in wisdom is kept safe.

Proverbs 28:26

God says to the snow, "Fall on the earth."

Job 37:6

A SNOWY WOODS

To me there's no more tranquil a scene than the woods behind our house covered in freshly-fallen snow. In the spring and summer, the woods is alive with the sounds of birds and animals and sprouting trees, and in the fall it crackles with the sound of dry leaves and animals scurrying to build nests and gather food. But in the winter the woods is silent and still, like a great cathedral before the worshipers arrive.

The wind may sway the tops of the trees, but there is little other movement. Once in a while a squirrel or rabbit ventures out for a quick look around but its footsteps make no sound in the fluffy snow. Deer come out as well, and they seem to look upon the snow with reverence. They step cautiously, silently. There's not even a sound when they nibble the withered vegetation that pokes above the drifts.

It seems it snows most during the night and it is a delight to awaken on a cold morning to an Ansel Adams-like scene out the bedroom window. Sometimes, though, snow falls during the day, landing lightly and drifting gently as if swept by the hand of God.

Walking in the snowy woods is calming. Soon you're stopped by the overwhelming majesty of the scene, awed by the oaks and maples and poplars and firs drooping with snow. You may see a red or yellow leaf glazed with ice and clinging to a branch, or even a tiny bud that mistakenly swelled up in a brief thaw.

A snowy woods shuts out the world and opens the mind and heart to the glory of God's creation. What a wonderful place to contemplate God, to talk to him, to marvel at the world he made for us, to pray.

Steven Cole

My soul finds rest in God alone.

Psalm 62:1

FIND A RESTING PLACE

Are you feeling overwhelmed today? Find a resting place. Even if it's just fifteen minutes in a quiet little nook where nobody will notice you, it will make a difference in your day. Ask God to recharge your batteries for the tasks that await you. Remember that he knows what is facing you, and he will give you strength to get through it.

Luci Swindoll

A man of understanding holds his tongue.

Proverbs 11:12

A BLESSED FOUNTAIN

My mother made it a habit every day, immediately after breakfast, to spend an hour in her room, reading the Bible, meditating over it, and praying to the Lord. That hour was like a blessed fountain from which she drew the strength and sweetness that prepared her to complete all her tasks. It also enabled her to maintain a genuine peacefulness in spite of the normal trying worries and pettiness that so often accompany life in a crowded neighborhood.

L.B. Cowman

They were glad when it grew calm.

Psalm 107:30

The Lord blesses his people with peace.

Psalm 29:11

SIMPLE, CALMING WORDS

The poor mulatto woman, whose simple faith had been well-nigh crushed and overwhelmed by the avalanche of cruelty and wrong which had fallen upon her, felt her soul raised up by the hymns and passages of Holy Writ, which [a] lowly missionary breathed into her ear in intervals, as they were going to and returning from work; and even the half-crazed and wandering mind of Cassy was soothed and calmed by his simple and unobtrusive influences.

Harriet Beecher Stowe

THE LORD'S PEACE

Circumstances today are far from rosy. The world finds itself in chaos. Many a family is in a crisis. The church is often at a loss for the right answers. Small wonder that our hearts lack peace and are full of uncertainty. But in spite of this we can experience the Lord's peace continually, and in every way.

Peace must be practical and practiced! We best begin each new day with God, reading his Word and praying. Then we can think back to this quiet time throughout the day to claim his peace when unrest and discord are knocking at our door. We must remind ourselves that no situation we find ourselves in is beyond the range of God's interest in us.

Gien Karssen

Jesus said, "Peace be with you!"

John 20:21

THE GIFT OF PEACE

The gift of peace can come quietly, unexpectedly—as you gaze at the soft glow of a candle during a hushed quiet time, as you walk in the woods and feel God close. It can come even in a glimpse out the window as your eye beholds the beauty outside. It can come through the loving gesture of a friend. It can come through laughter, or tears, or simply silence. It can come through prayer.

Betsy Lee

My God turns my darkness into light.

Psalm 18:28

PITCH DARK!

Cave tours often include a time when the guide turns out the lights. You cannot imagine such pitch darkness as you experience for that brief moment deep within the earth. You think, "This is what it must have been like before God created the universe."

Once, while touring a cave in northern Mexico the lights went out due to a power failure. Curiously, no one panicked. There was dead silence, not a word was spoken. No one coughed. After what seemed an eternity, but was perhaps only a minute, the lights came on. I thought I was probably the only one who felt God's closeness during that time of darkness, but I was wrong. When we emerged from the cave a man behind me said to his wife, "We must thank God for being with us in the darkness," and he made the sign of the cross.

Steven Cole

GOD SPOKE, "REMEMBER THE SABBATH DAY
BY KEEPING IT HOLY.

Six days you shall labor and do all your work, but the seventh day is a Sabbath to the Lord your God. On it you shall not do any work, neither you, nor your son or daughter, nor your manservant or maidservant, nor your animals, nor the alien within your gates. For in six days the Lord made the heavens and the earth, the sea, and all that is in them, but he rested on the seventh day. Therefore the Lord blessed the Sabbath day and made it holy."

Exodus 20: 8-11

Let the peace of Christ rule in your hearts.

Colossians 3:15

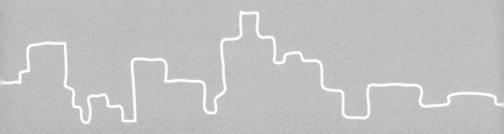

TAKE A VACATION!

We need to refresh ourselves to maintain physical and spiritual strength. Our schedules are demanding. They drain our physical, mental, emotional, and spiritual life. God's Holy Spirit gives us strength for his schedule for us. I believe God plans for us to include times of rest and relaxation in our schedule. Our rest times may consist of a vacation where we can relax with a change of environment, or simply a respite right where we are. Either way, time spent with the Lord brings renewal and refreshment.

Millie Stamm

SLOW ME DOWN, LORD

Ease the rushing of my steps by the hushing of my heart.

Slow me down, Lord, amid the confusion of my day.

Draw me in as I cast anchor to repair and restore.

Help me to remember that happiness is not a pursuit

toward an end, a place to finally arrive.

It comes as I spend a few moments a day

reflecting on the things that make my soul thrive.

Jan Coleman

Jesus got up, rebuked the wind and said to the waves, "Quiet! Be Still!" Then the wind died down and it was completely calm.

Mark 4:39

EYE OF THE STORM

Hurricanes are simply very high speed winds blowing in a circle around a low pressure center called the eye of the storm. Hurricane winds can reach 150 mph or more, but in the eye there is dead calm because centrifugal force keeps the high speed wind from being drawn into it.

Often our lives are in such turmoil that we feel we are in a hurricane of problems. We may be beset with fear, guilt, shame or self-doubt, all leading to frustration and indecision. But God is the eye of our stormy lives. Take his outstretched hand and let him pull you into his calm and loving presence. With God you can weather any storm.

Steven Cole

The Lord said, "My Presence will go with you, and I will give you rest."

Exodus 33:14

Excerpts contained in this book were pulled from the following resources:

Briscoe, Jill. *Spiritual Arts*. Grand Rapids: Zondervan, 2007.

Cowman, L.B. *Streams in the Desert*. Grand Rapids: Zondervan, 1996.

_____. *God's Word of Life for Women*. Grand Rapids: Zondervan, 1997.

_____. *Joy for a Woman's Soul*. Grand Rapids: Zondervan, 1998.

_____. *More Soul Retreats for Women*. Grand Rapids: Zondervan, 2003.

Mulholland, M. Robert Jr. *Invitation to a Journey*. Westmont: InterVarsity Press, 1993. Used by
    permission of InterVarsity Press, P.O. Box 1400, Downers Grove, IL 60515. www.ivpress.com.

Ortberg, John. *The Life You've Always Wanted*. Grand Rapids: Zondervan, 1997, 2002.

Ortberg, John. *Love Beyond Reason*. Grand Rapids: Zondervan, 1998.

Ortberg, John. *When the Game Is Over, It All Goes Back in the Box*. Grand Rapids: Zondervan, 2007.

Rich, Ronda. *What Southern Women Know about Faith*. Grand Rapids: Zondervan, 2009.

_____. *Simple Gifts: Unwrapping the Special Moments of Everyday Life*. Grand Rapids: Zondervan, 1999.

Sittser, Gerald L. *A Grace Disguised*. Grand Rapids: Zondervan, 1995, 2004.

_____. *Soul Retreats for Busy People*. Grand Rapids: Zondervan, 2002.

_____. *Soul Retreats for Leaders*. Grand Rapids: Zondervan, 2003.

_____. *Soul Retreats for Students*. Grand Rapids: Zondervan, 2003.

_____. *Soul Retreats for Teachers*. Grand Rapids: Zondervan, 2002.

Stirling, Roz. *Breakfast with God Volume 3*. Grand Rapids: Zondervan, 2000.

Stowe, Harriet Beecher. *Uncle Tom's Cabin*. Cambridge: Houghton, Mifflin and Company, 1851,
    1878, 1879.

Trembley, David and Lo-Ann. *The Gratitude Attitude*. Grand Rapids: Zondervan, 2003.

Walsh, Sheila. *Honestly*. Grand Rapids: Zondervan, 2006.